LAUGHTER
JOURNAL

30 DAY
LAUGHTER THERAPY
CHALLENGE

INSTRUCTIONS: Once or twice a day, record everything that has made you laugh – even if it is just a small giggle. At the end of the day, add up and record how many times you laughed on that day. Then take some time to reflect on any common themes or people, and journal how the laughter made you feel and affected your mood.

First Edition: 2020

LAUGHTER CHALLENGE: day 1

What really made me laugh today?

Small things I found amusing:

_____

_____

_____

_____

_____

Belly laughs:

_____

_____

_____

_____

_____

_____

_____

_____

_____

Times I Laughed Today: Overall Mood:

How did the laughter affect my overall mood?

Laughter Themes

_____

_____

_____

_____

_____

_____

_____

People Who Made Me Laugh

_____

_____

_____

_____

_____

_____

_____

What did the laughter mean to me?

LAUGHTER CHALLENGE: day 2

What really made me laugh today?

Small things I found amusing:

_____

_____

_____

_____

_____

Belly laughs:

_____

_____

_____

_____

_____

_____

_____

_____

Times I Laughed Today: _____   Overall Mood: _____

How did the laughter affect my overall mood?

Laughter Themes

_____

_____

_____

_____

_____

_____

_____

People Who Made Me Laugh

_____

_____

_____

_____

_____

_____

_____

What did the laughter mean to me?

LAUGHTER CHALLENGE: day 3

What really made me laugh today?

Small things I found amusing:

_____

_____

_____

_____

_____

Belly laughs:

_____

_____

_____

_____

_____

_____

_____

_____

Times I Laughed Today: Overall Mood:

How did the laughter affect my overall mood?

Laughter Themes

_____

_____

_____

_____

_____

_____

_____

_____

People Who Made Me Laugh

_____

_____

_____

_____

_____

_____

_____

What did the laughter mean to me?

LAUGHTER CHALLENGE: day 4

What really made me laugh today?

Small things I found amusing:

_____

_____

_____

_____

_____

_____

_____

Belly laughs:

_____

_____

_____

_____

_____

_____

_____

_____

_____

_____

Times I Laughed Today: Overall Mood:

How did the laughter affect my overall mood?

Laughter Themes

_____

_____

_____

_____

_____

_____

_____

People Who Made Me Laugh

_____

_____

_____

_____

_____

_____

_____

What did the laughter mean to me?

LAUGHTER CHALLENGE: day 5

What really made me laugh today?

Small things I found amusing:

_____

_____

_____

_____

_____

Belly laughs:

_____

_____

_____

_____

_____

_____

_____

_____

Times I Laughed Today: Overall Mood:

How did the laughter affect my overall mood?

Laughter Themes

_____

_____

_____

_____

_____

_____

_____

People Who Made Me Laugh

_____

_____

_____

_____

_____

_____

_____

What did the laughter mean to me?

LAUGHTER CHALLENGE: day 6

What really made me laugh today?

Small things I found amusing:

_____

_____

_____

_____

_____

Belly laughs:

_____

_____

_____

_____

_____

_____

_____

_____

_____

Times I Laughed Today: Overall Mood:

How did the laughter affect my overall mood?

Laughter Themes

_____

_____

_____

_____

_____

_____

_____

People Who Made Me Laugh

_____

_____

_____

_____

_____

_____

_____

What did the laughter mean to me?

LAUGHTER CHALLENGE: day 7

What really made me laugh today?

Small things I found amusing:

_____

_____

_____

_____

_____

_____

Belly laughs:

_____

_____

_____

_____

_____

_____

_____

_____

_____

Times I Laughed Today: Overall Mood:

How did the laughter affect my overall mood?

Laughter Themes

_____

_____

_____

_____

_____

_____

_____

People Who Made Me Laugh

_____

_____

_____

_____

_____

_____

What did the laughter mean to me?

LAUGHTER CHALLENGE: day 8

What really made me laugh today?

Small things I found amusing:

_____

_____

_____

_____

_____

Belly laughs:

_____

_____

_____

_____

_____

_____

_____

_____

Times I Laughed Today: Overall Mood:

How did the laughter affect my overall mood?

Laughter Themes

_____

_____

_____

_____

_____

_____

_____

People Who Made Me Laugh

_____

_____

_____

_____

_____

_____

_____

What did the laughter mean to me?

LAUGHTER CHALLENGE: day 9

What really made me laugh today?

Small things I found amusing:

_____

_____

_____

_____

_____

Belly laughs:

_____

_____

_____

_____

_____

_____

_____

_____

Times I Laughed Today: Overall Mood:

How did the laughter affect my overall mood?

Laughter Themes

_____

_____

_____

_____

_____

_____

_____

People Who Made Me Laugh

_____

_____

_____

_____

_____

_____

_____

What did the laughter mean to me?

LAUGHTER CHALLENGE: day 10

What really made me laugh today?

Small things I found amusing:

_____

_____

_____

_____

_____

Belly laughs:

_____

_____

_____

_____

_____

_____

_____

_____

Times I Laughed Today: Overall Mood:

How did the laughter affect my overall mood?

Laughter Themes

_____

_____

_____

_____

_____

_____

_____

People Who Made Me Laugh

_____

_____

_____

_____

_____

_____

_____

What did the laughter mean to me?

LAUGHTER CHALLENGE: day 11

What really made me laugh today?

Small things I found amusing:

_____

_____

_____

_____

_____

Belly laughs:

_____

_____

_____

_____

_____

_____

_____

_____

Times I Laughed Today: _____   Overall Mood: _____

How did the laughter affect my overall mood?

Laughter Themes

_____

_____

_____

_____

_____

_____

_____

People Who Made Me Laugh

_____

_____

_____

_____

_____

_____

_____

What did the laughter mean to me?

LAUGHTER CHALLENGE: day 12

What really made me laugh today?

Small things I found amusing:

_____

_____

_____

_____

_____

Belly laughs:

_____

_____

_____

_____

_____

_____

_____

_____

_____

Times I Laughed Today: Overall Mood:

How did the laughter affect my overall mood?

Laughter Themes

_____

_____

_____

_____

_____

_____

_____

People Who Made Me Laugh

_____

_____

_____

_____

_____

_____

_____

What did the laughter mean to me?

LAUGHTER CHALLENGE: day 13

What really made me laugh today?

Small things I found amusing:

_____

_____

_____

_____

_____

_____

Belly laughs:

_____

_____

_____

_____

_____

_____

_____

_____

_____

Times I Laughed Today: Overall Mood:

How did the laughter affect my overall mood?

Laughter Themes

_____

_____

_____

_____

_____

_____

_____

People Who Made Me Laugh

_____

_____

_____

_____

_____

_____

_____

What did the laughter mean to me?

LAUGHTER CHALLENGE: day 14

What really made me laugh today?

Small things I found amusing:

_____

_____

_____

_____

_____

Belly laughs:

_____

_____

_____

_____

_____

_____

_____

_____

Times I Laughed Today: Overall Mood:

How did the laughter affect my overall mood?

Laughter Themes

_____

_____

_____

_____

_____

_____

_____

People Who Made Me Laugh

_____

_____

_____

_____

_____

_____

_____

What did the laughter mean to me?

LAUGHTER CHALLENGE: day 15

What really made me laugh today?

Small things I found amusing:

_____

_____

_____

_____

_____

Belly laughs:

_____

_____

_____

_____

_____

_____

_____

_____

Times I Laughed Today: Overall Mood:

How did the laughter affect my overall mood?

Laughter Themes

_____

_____

_____

_____

_____

_____

_____

People Who Made Me Laugh

_____

_____

_____

_____

_____

_____

_____

What did the laughter mean to me?

LAUGHTER CHALLENGE: day 16

What really made me laugh today?

Small things I found amusing:

_____

_____

_____

_____

_____

Belly laughs:

_____

_____

_____

_____

_____

_____

_____

_____

_____

Times I Laughed Today: Overall Mood:

How did the laughter affect my overall mood?

Laughter Themes

_____

_____

_____

_____

_____

_____

_____

People Who Made Me Laugh

_____

_____

_____

_____

_____

_____

_____

What did the laughter mean to me?

LAUGHTER CHALLENGE: day 17

What really made me laugh today?

Small things I found amusing:

_____

_____

_____

_____

_____

Belly laughs:

_____

_____

_____

_____

_____

_____

_____

_____

Times I Laughed Today: Overall Mood:

How did the laughter affect my overall mood?

Laughter Themes

_____

_____

_____

_____

_____

_____

_____

People Who Made Me Laugh

_____

_____

_____

_____

_____

_____

_____

What did the laughter mean to me?

LAUGHTER CHALLENGE: day 18

What really made me laugh today?

Small things I found amusing:

_____

_____

_____

_____

_____

Belly laughs:

_____

_____

_____

_____

_____

_____

_____

_____

_____

Times I Laughed Today: Overall Mood:

How did the laughter affect my overall mood?

Laughter Themes

_____

_____

_____

_____

_____

_____

_____

People Who Made Me Laugh

_____

_____

_____

_____

_____

_____

_____

What did the laughter mean to me?

LAUGHTER CHALLENGE: day 19

What really made me laugh today?

Small things I found amusing:

_____

_____

_____

_____

_____

Belly laughs:

_____

_____

_____

_____

_____

_____

_____

_____

Times I Laughed Today: Overall Mood:

How did the laughter affect my overall mood?

Laughter Themes

_____

_____

_____

_____

_____

_____

_____

People Who Made Me Laugh

_____

_____

_____

_____

_____

_____

_____

What did the laughter mean to me?

LAUGHTER CHALLENGE: day 20

What really made me laugh today?

Small things I found amusing:

_____

_____

_____

_____

_____

Belly laughs:

_____

_____

_____

_____

_____

_____

_____

_____

Times I Laughed Today: _____   Overall Mood: _____

How did the laughter affect my overall mood?

Laughter Themes

_____

_____

_____

_____

_____

_____

_____

People Who Made Me Laugh

_____

_____

_____

_____

_____

_____

_____

What did the laughter mean to me?

LAUGHTER CHALLENGE: day 21

What really made me laugh today?

Small things I found amusing:

_____

_____

_____

_____

_____

_____

Belly laughs:

_____

_____

_____

_____

_____

_____

_____

_____

_____

Times I Laughed Today: Overall Mood:

How did the laughter affect my overall mood?

Laughter Themes

_____

_____

_____

_____

_____

_____

_____

People Who Made Me Laugh

_____

_____

_____

_____

_____

_____

_____

What did the laughter mean to me?

LAUGHTER CHALLENGE: day 22

What really made me laugh today?

Small things I found amusing:

_____

_____

_____

_____

_____

Belly laughs:

_____

_____

_____

_____

_____

_____

_____

_____

Times I Laughed Today: _____ Overall Mood: _____

How did the laughter affect my overall mood?

Laughter Themes

_____

_____

_____

_____

_____

_____

_____

People Who Made Me Laugh

_____

_____

_____

_____

_____

_____

_____

What did the laughter mean to me?

LAUGHTER CHALLENGE: day 23

What really made me laugh today?

Small things I found amusing:

_____

_____

_____

_____

_____

Belly laughs:

_____

_____

_____

_____

_____

_____

_____

_____

Times I Laughed Today: Overall Mood:

How did the laughter affect my overall mood?

Laughter Themes

_____

_____

_____

_____

_____

_____

_____

People Who Made Me Laugh

_____

_____

_____

_____

_____

_____

_____

What did the laughter mean to me?

LAUGHTER CHALLENGE: day 24

What really made me laugh today?

Small things I found amusing:

_____

_____

_____

_____

_____

_____

Belly laughs:

_____

_____

_____

_____

_____

_____

_____

_____

_____

Times I Laughed Today: Overall Mood:

How did the laughter affect my overall mood?

Laughter Themes

_____
_____
_____
_____
_____
_____
_____

People Who Made Me Laugh

_____
_____
_____
_____
_____
_____
_____

What did the laughter mean to me?

LAUGHTER CHALLENGE: day 25

What really made me laugh today?

Small things I found amusing:

_____

_____

_____

_____

_____

Belly laughs:

_____

_____

_____

_____

_____

_____

_____

_____

Times I Laughed Today: _____ Overall Mood: _____

How did the laughter affect my overall mood?

Laughter Themes	People Who Made Me Laugh
_____	_____
_____	_____
_____	_____
_____	_____
_____	_____
_____	_____
_____	_____

What did the laughter mean to me?

LAUGHTER CHALLENGE: day 26

What really made me laugh today?

Small things I found amusing:

_____

_____

_____

_____

_____

Belly laughs:

_____

_____

_____

_____

_____

_____

_____

_____

_____

Times I Laughed Today: Overall Mood:

How did the laughter affect my overall mood?

Laughter Themes

_____

_____

_____

_____

_____

_____

People Who Made Me Laugh

_____

_____

_____

_____

_____

_____

What did the laughter mean to me?

LAUGHTER CHALLENGE: day 27

What really made me laugh today?

Small things I found amusing:

_____

_____

_____

_____

_____

Belly laughs:

_____

_____

_____

_____

_____

_____

_____

_____

_____

Times I Laughed Today: Overall Mood:

How did the laughter affect my overall mood?

Laughter Themes

_____

_____

_____

_____

_____

_____

_____

People Who Made Me Laugh

_____

_____

_____

_____

_____

_____

_____

What did the laughter mean to me?

LAUGHTER CHALLENGE: day 28

What really made me laugh today?

Small things I found amusing:

_____

_____

_____

_____

_____

Belly laughs:

_____

_____

_____

_____

_____

_____

_____

_____

_____

Times I Laughed Today: Overall Mood:

How did the laughter affect my overall mood?

Laughter Themes

_____

_____

_____

_____

_____

_____

_____

People Who Made Me Laugh

_____

_____

_____

_____

_____

_____

_____

What did the laughter mean to me?

LAUGHTER CHALLENGE: day 29

What really made me laugh today?

Small things I found amusing:

_____

_____

_____

_____

_____

Belly laughs:

_____

_____

_____

_____

_____

_____

_____

_____

Times I Laughed Today: Overall Mood:

How did the laughter affect my overall mood?

Laughter Themes

_____

_____

_____

_____

_____

_____

_____

People Who Made Me Laugh

_____

_____

_____

_____

_____

_____

_____

What did the laughter mean to me?

LAUGHTER CHALLENGE: day 30

What really made me laugh today?

Small things I found amusing:

_____

_____

_____

_____

_____

Belly laughs:

_____

_____

_____

_____

_____

_____

_____

_____

Times I Laughed Today: Overall Mood:

How did the laughter affect my overall mood?

Laughter Themes

_____

_____

_____

_____

_____

_____

_____

People Who Made Me Laugh

_____

_____

_____

_____

_____

_____

_____

What did the laughter mean to me?

30 DAY LAUGHTER CHALLENGE CONCLUSIONS

What recurring themes and/or people made me laugh most often?

_____

_____

_____

_____

_____

How would I describe my sense of humor?

_____

_____

_____

What small things in my life bring me joy?

_____

_____

_____

_____

_____

Times I Laughed This Month: _____

It's time to
CHANGE YOUR **MINDSET!**

FOCUS ON THE THINGS
that
MAKE YOU **HAPPY**
and
FOCUS LESS ON
WHAT MAKES YOU SAD.

IMPLEMENTATION

PLANS & NOTES

IMPLEMENTATION

PLANS & NOTES

IMPLEMENTATION

PLANS & NOTES

I DID IT!!!!!

Made in United States
Orlando, FL
02 September 2024

51042804R00039